h is for human

emotional
stories from
america's
schools.

by: k. a.
campion

Susan –
Thank you for
reading and
fighting the
fighting the
good fight
too !

Kelly

For –

My children,
and the others
who call me
Mom.

And for my one
true love, J.

ubuntu.

The following stories have been etched in my soul for years. I've carried them with me through classrooms, across thousands of miles, and into the raising of my own children.

I've felt every one of the emotions in the following pages, and continue to do so each day when I arrive at my school. It keeps my life interesting, to say the least.

The kids I've had the fortune to teach have made me a more sensitive human. I tell their stories when I am able to, and when it's appropriate.

Teaching changes a person.

I hope if you're reading this and you aren't a teacher, these stories touch you, or inspire you to make a change.

These kids live in your neighborhood. They play sports with your kids. They sleep in your houses. They eat your food. They get called fuck-ups, poor kids, "those kids," kids you avoid talking to. They pass you in hoodies on the street. They are every shade of brown, black, and white.

They aren't always treated as such, but

They Are Humans.

Aren't we all?

Table of Contents

***The author writes under a pseudonym to protect her identity, as she still works in classrooms.

***Gender pronouns and locations have been altered to protect the identity of the humans in each story.

***A majority of the proceeds made from the sale of this book will go directly to the subjects addressed in the stories.

PREFACE:

I'll be honest...

I've struggled with the challenge of writing this book. It wasn't easy to tell stories about kids I've worked with over the years. I worried about coming off as a

"white savior"

I assure you...I wish I could be considered a *savior* in some sense, but alas, I am a human too.

It's true, I am white. Some of these kids aren't. Some are. To me, they're

simply *humans*.

Struggling through their teen years.

That, in itself, is pretty universal.

I work hard to be an includer. To be sensitive. To <u>learn</u> more.

And I encourage my students, and you as a reader, to do the same.

A

is

for

Appreciation

I called you Portland before you even arrived in my class. You were there for the first week of school visiting a mother who hasn't much to do with you. I'd learn that later, of course.

The year you were in my class wasn't an easy one. Your friends gave me a run for my money. But you. You were different.

We clicked pretty quickly. Perhaps it was over the knife you brought to school that kept me up all night. I cried, not wanting you to be suspended. You hugged *me* and told *me* it was okay. You kept my head above water more than you know.

I learned about your sensitive side. You don't share that with anyone. I learned about the dad you have little connection with. A mom you never really talk to. The sisters who care for you. The five years you were sent to Mexico for grandparents to raise you.

And the *terrible* thing that happened to you.

I learned you push it all down. And refuse to talk about it often. It won't define you.

Soccer defines you. I could watch you play all day long, and have. And I don't even love soccer. But I've become your biggest fan.

The night I left, we had a bonfire on the beach. Just a small group of us. You laid in the sand and I knew you were sad. Everyone was crying. But not you.

You won't cry.

And for some reason that bothered me.

But I drove you home last. Because if *you* didn't cry, I knew that *I* would.

I parked the car, turned it off. And you made a noise beside me. I heard you crying. And you said words that

Broke My Fucking Heart.

"It feels like I'm losing my mom."

For the next hour and a half, we cried. Because it felt like I was saying goodbye to my son.

I was sick for days. I stared out the window, trying to figure out how I could get you here.

But you're 1200 miles away, and it breaks my heart.

Every. Single. Day.

Of *all* the kids...*you* are mine.

The thing about teaching is…it
makes the world smaller.

I'm not sure why running into my
kids all over the place has become
such a gift, but it has.

I walked into the restaurant where
you work, and you said, "Hi, K!"

We exchanged hugs, and smiles.

I realized we knew a lot about each
other's lives, thanks to social media.

Thank you, seriously.

You're a mother now. We both are.

I walked out, telling my son who
you are. He's five.

"I taught her 15 years ago!"
surprising myself too.

"Whoa! That's a lonnnng time,
Mommy.

"She's nice."

Yes, yes she is.

I had a smile on my face all day.
Such a simple moment.

You - selling me a loaf of fresh
bread, and pastries.

You're an adult now. We both are.
We walk in the same world.

Two humans.

Two mothers.

I'm thankful for this.

All of this.

I've got this, you tell the waiter
after I've ordered food to go.

Look at you, all grown up, and
buying *me* a drink. And now dinner.

You're wearing a suit, selling
Bimmers in Queens.

You're wearing a suit. And nice
shoes.

And we're sitting in a bar.

In Brooklyn,

reminiscing about your classmates.

This one's a parent, this one's in jail,
this one and that one and this one
and that one.

I knew you wouldn't take that
route.

You were sensitive as a kid.

You gave me a stuffed bunny once,
and I kept it all those years until I
had a child of my own.

I gave it to her. And I told her about
you.

You're calling me by my first name
and talking like an adult, and I am
struggling to contain my pride.
You've grown into quite a man.

A man.

You're a man now.

It doesn't mean much to you, it's
just life. But to me, it means
everything.

You've traveled.

Stayed humble.

Taken care of your family.

That rabbit you gave me has moved
all over the country and back again.
Stuffed in boxes. Cuddled by my
kids. It has sustained through it all.
It's still the soft, gorgeous plush it
was when you shyly handed it to
me all those years ago.

What a metaphor, no?

Thanks for the drink, kid.

B
is
for
Blunt

December 2003. Graduate.
Teaching license. Go forth.

Do your thing.

Save them all.

I knew I wasn't going to save them all, but my mantra was/is,

"I'll die trying."

All the books, the group projects, the mock lesson plans couldn't have prepared me for my first job as a substitute.

I got there early, of course. I was wearing ironed khakis. God. And a button up shirt, white with stripes? From New York and Co. Sensible flats. Probably a modest amount of jewelry, and a new, shiny engagement ring.

I couldn't have looked more out of place.

More white.

I was thrust a set of keys, pushed into a room, and told,

GOOD LUCK.

The bell rang and the butterflies started swirling.

I wasn't so naïve; I knew it was just a sub job.

I attempted to pick up where the teacher, out for a, get this…

mental breakdown, left off.

"Don't know when she's coming back…Or if."

I begin. Talking. Rushing. And they begin…

Talking.

I ask a girl to please be quiet.

"Fuck you, white bitch."

You should try being a little

less...

sarcastic-

A mentor once said to me.

I smiled.

But-

That's my superpower.

c
is
for
cynical

I wrote letters to the class to introduce myself, and asked that they write me a letter back.

"I hate English class," you wrote. You were adamant about disliking English and writing and reading.

Set on it.

Matter of fact.

I was intimidated, truthfully. What a bold statement for a seemingly-pleasant white girl, from middle America.

You didn't look edgy, or defiant. More country, and compliant.

And you were. But you gave me a run for my money,

with your *silence*.

And at the end of the semester...

"This was my favorite class. I actually like reading and writing now."

You became a teacher.

I hope you receive this gift too.

Career day. A day when I don't have to plan, and get to sit back and listen.

NOPE.

Several years ago, sitting in the back of my room, I watched as two 20-something-white-girls-in-heels-with-makeup-and-highlights...

Walked

Confidently

Into

My

Room.

"We're in cosmetic marketing."

Blank stares.

They proceeded, bless their hearts, to keep talking about marketing makeup to kids who didn't know where their next meal was coming from.

These are the kids marketing takes advantage of.

Two boys sitting in front of me must have had some beef going between them that day. Nothing was really said, but all of a sudden,

RIGHT BEFORE MY EYES

Two bodies, on the floor, desks and chairs

Flying

Punching

Spit

Screaming

I ushered kids out of the room, as per protocol.

Then attempted to break them up.

The poor girls were horrified.

Pretty sure the girls

Walked

Confidently

Out

Of

My

Room.

All before lunch.

_____

D

is

for

Disgust

A long time ago you came to me and told me what he was doing to your sister.

"Last night he tried to do it to me."

CPS was called, and they failed you.

Eventually, a sibling ratted him out and he was "taken away."

We spent a Saturday traipsing through Manhattan to find you a prom dress for your 8th grade prom.

We ate at Chipotle somewhere near 23rd street, and faced the windows on barstools. You were elated to have attention, and walk through the city.

We found you a dress, and you wore a different one to the prom anyway. You saved our dress for graduation.

When you told me about your first high school boyfriend, and how he took your virginity one night, I cried with you. I'd never felt so protective over a student before.

The drink, a slip of a pill. You waking up in his bed, with blood between your naked legs.

I walked you straight to the precinct after school. The detectives notably Irish, in a Dominican and Puerto Rican neighborhood.

"Excuse me? Miss? Can I just ask, what the hell are *you* doing here?" in his Brooklyn-Irish accent. "Do your *parents* know where you teach?"

As if I wasn't supposed to be there. Because why? I'm white? From the Midwest?

They failed to find your boyfriend. He'd done this to others. You weren't his first, but,

HE WAS YOURS.

Things changed with you after that. Sex wasn't so sacred.

You have a beautiful daughter that you are raising now. And you look like the model you always wanted to be.

I sincerely hope that the demons in your past are gone. That you raise a fierce daughter.

Your innocence was stolen more than once, and I couldn't stop it.

Halloween is gang initiation day in some neighborhoods.

I cannot confirm this, as I haven't seen it in person.

I did not deal with gangs while growing up.

On Halloween of my first year, I learned we were having an early-rapid-release.

That sounds like a medication.

It wasn't.

We were told to talk to kids about going straight home.

I was worried. I walked to the train rapidly and back to the safety of my own neighborhood.

Naïve.

Privileged.

I know this.

I did ask my kids before we left how many of them knew someone who had been killed, or badly hurt, by gang activity.

And don't you know it,

My

Entire

Class raised their hands.

Imagine my surprise, when they asked how many people I knew.

None.

E

is

for

Encouraged

Some time, years back, I decided that my students needed access to better books. I couldn't afford to keep buying them. And it was hard to keep up.

I made a list one day.

Stood in Barnes and Nobel and wrote down all the books I wanted to give access to my kids.

I didn't really know what to do with it. Just had a legal pad of paper full of books I wished I could put in my classroom.

And then I had a thought:

Make a wish list. Put it on Amazon.

Ask my friends on Facebook to donate a book.

HUNDREDS of books showed up on my doorstep over the next few weeks.

EVERY book I asked for (and more) showed up in boxes.

I think the best part was bringing the books to school to share with the kids.

It wasn't the reading that was the most important, though.

They learned that people, all over the WORLD cared enough to send them books.

They started asking me about the people who donated.

How do you know them?

I wrote the name and city/state/country of the donors in the inside cover of each book.

I've done this three times now. I have more books than I can count.

And yes, the reading is important. I'll never deny that.

But the looks on their faces when I tell them who and where the book is from.

Priceless.

A group of girls in my class wanted to read the book, <u>Sisterhood of the Traveling Pants</u> by Ann Brashears, when it first came out.

My co-teacher and I had read it and started passing it around to some girls in our class.

After a good amount of girls had finished the book, we learned that the movie was coming out.

We decided to take the girls to Brooklyn to see the film.

A group of nearly 10 of us took the train to the theater one evening, after school.

As new teachers, this was a bit out of range of our budget, but we didn't care. Kids were reading, and we were going to reward them for that.

Before we left, my principal handed me cash and told me to get popcorn and snacks for all of the girls.

I was elated.

The movie was good, and the girls loved being spoiled.

My favorite point was looking down the row, through tears, and seeing that every single girl was crying at the same time.

It's funny, because we were broke. We didn't have the money to be taking the kids to the movies.

We were barely squeaking out enough money for rent.

But when my co-teacher and I looked at one another, through tears,

The money didn't matter.

And in this job, it usually doesn't.

F
is
for
Furious

The 2004 school year opened after Labor Day, but only for two days. There were Jewish holidays we had off for.

That was new for me. But I was ready for a break after two days.

I was informed by a person who would make my life a living hell, that my classroom needed decorating.

I had no money. I had no idea where to buy teaching "stuff"

I had no money.

I got creative that four day weekend. I improvised. As teachers do.

A word wall, I was told. You need a word wall. And something on your door!

After unloading the boxes into our apartment on the east side, I started tracing stars. I cut out 26 stars for each letter of the alphabet. I covered them in tinfoil.

Monday morning came around, and I bounded up the 5 flights of stairs to decorate my room before the kids arrived.

The door was shining in tin foil and signs. The word wall was decorated.

It looked like we were starting to have a classroom.

The kids arrived and were in awe.

They. Loved. It.

Midway through the morning, and
my teaching, the person who
directed me to decorate my room
was talking outside my door.

R
 I
   P
    P
     P
      P
       P
       I
        N
         G.

This

is

just

the

beginning.

I hear it, but try to keep teaching, as
though my class can't hear the
tearing of the entire front of my
door off.

Marching in, they walk to the back
of the room and tear a good 18 feet
of paper down.

My word wall. OUR word wall.

Sitting in a garbage can at the front
of my classroom.

Kids gasp, talking, whispering.

I stare, lump in my throat.

I WILL NOT CRY IN FRONT OF KIDS.

I WILL NOT CRY.

I WILL NOT CRY.

"Why aren't they quiet?!"

"What are you teaching?!"

It's shrill and it's as bad as it sounds.

Her first general education class.

Mine.

No pressure.

She's severely autistic, they said.

But she has a 1:1 aid with her all day.

Well, not first period. The aid informed me that her hours don't start until 40 minutes into a 50-minute period.

That's not helpful.

I did my best to keep support staff aware of what was happening in my class. Calendars were sent out. Assignments emailed to everyone involved.

But English classes are often a challenge for an Autistic student.

Getting into a character's head? Asking for the reasons a character did something?

Her aid informed me that she wrote the papers and the student typed them.

Mother insists on A's.

Huh?

But?

Now I'm sitting here, grading the writing of my colleague.

How is this helping?

How is *any* of this helping?

G

is

for

Guilt

Overheard by an admin in my school-from-hell.

Yelling down the hall to "motivate" kids to get to class-

WHY ARE YOU SMILING? THIS IS SCHOOL. WE DON'T HAVE FUN HERE! GET TO CLASS!

I turned on my heel, because you're kidding.

Right?

Wrong.

A month later, the same admin walks into my freezing classroom to a class full of students-

Working.

They were wearing winter coats.

It was cold.

When asked why they were wearing their coats, I responded,

It's cold. I asked them to take the coats off, but they refused. And, it's cold.

I had a letter in my mailbox that afternoon. It's the only time I've ever been "written up" in my life.

Letting students wear winter coats in class-

GUILTY AS CHARGED.

Shame on me for thinking that reaching out to the people who are supposed to take care of you, would.

Your grades were good, but starting to slip.

The boyfriend, a year older, started walking you to classes and you'd come in a minute late.

Saying good bye with a kiss in the hall.

Eventually, after several warnings, I figured a parental reinforcement would help.

I couldn't have been more wrong.

I called and let them know that I was worried. Your grades were slipping a bit, and perhaps you just needed some kind of reminder as to why you were in school in the first place.

What was I hoping they would do?

You went home that night and came back too quiet the next day.

In second period you pulled up a shirt sleeve to reveal a nightmare.

A classmate saw and told the counselor.

In her office you revealed the *reinforcement* from the night before.

An extension cord.

"She stopped, eventually," you said, about your mother, who whipped you with the cord.

"And then he started," you said about your father, who continued the lashes.

Your legs, front and back.

Your arms.

Your back.

The worst thing I've ever seen, the counselor informed me.

CPS took you and your siblings away the following night, after a trip to the hospital.

You were in foster care while your parents spent time in jail, and were allowed to see you with visitation.

Eventually, you were reunited. Things were better, you promised.

The scars, undoubtable on your skin.

The horror, I would never forget. It's rare I call to report behavior to parents anymore.

How can I be sure you'll be safe?

How do I trust parents who say, "We'll take care of it."?

You walked in to my 8th grade room with a scowl and a tattoo. You were 16 and angry. It was later in the year, and the rumors swirled as to why you transferred to our school.

"Is he in a gang?!" And you didn't respond. You didn't really talk. And for that very reason, I took to you. I made it my mission to save you that year. You stopped coming to school, but would sneak up the five stories of stairs to dip into my classroom. I can only assume you felt safe there, but you just said, "I like this class."

I dreamt about how I could save you. I could see the anger in your clenched fists, your dark eyes staring straight ahead.

The school failed you. They didn't see a sweet boy, but a criminal. A truant. You made the numbers look bad.

And one day, you couldn't take it and punched a window with wire in the glass. It split your knuckles to hamburger. You went to the hospital, and were promptly expelled.

I never saw you again.

Are you okay?

Good luck with that kid.

I was honestly scared with all that I had heard when you walked into my class.

But charisma! You've got that on lock.

And I quickly see how you do not really read well, and you've been in special education classes your entire life. And math isn't your favorite either. And now that I think about it, your words come out jumbled sometimes when you speak, and you're excited.

Defense.

I've seen this a number of times.

You're cute, and you use that. You flirt with all the girls, *and* the female teachers.

You're funny.

You read people, not books.

School is not for you, and you're getting by as best you can. You know when to cool it, but you rarely do. And suspensions are a joke.

"I'll go to work with my dad," you tell me. And make money. Why would you bother coming to school?

It kills me that your ability to read people cannot be assessed and put on a report card. Instead you read F's down each column.

I want to tell you that your Spanish, caramel skin, and dimples will get you far. I want to tell you that your ability to make others feel good, and laugh, makes you someone everyone wants to be around.

Instead I roll my eyes when you get caught stoned at school, and tell you to quit drinking on campus.

I get it. You want to fail to prove everyone right. But you and I both know they are wrong about you.

How did I lose you? My head swirls when I try to imagine where you ended up.

Are you in jail? Married? A father? Working? College?

You were always special to me. I suppose that is why I am writing about you here.

You were tall, for an 8th grader. Your skin was iced coffee, and your hair was frizzy. Full lips, and bright white teeth, with an infectious smile.

You tried to be tough, but broke down and cried like a small child on occasion.

I thought of you often after we parted ways in June of 2006. You marched out the door in a cap and gown, and I didn't see you again.

Gone.

I heard you moved to North Carolina to be near the father you longed for, but who had never been a part of your life. Your young, gorgeous mother must have been heart-broken.

I was driving one day, and you walked right out in the cross walk. Just poof! You literally appeared out of nowhere. You looked right at me, and I jumped out of my car to hug you.

We exchanged stories, and promises to bump into one another again.

And again, you marched into the Brooklyn air, and disappeared, wearing a security uniform.

Just like graduation day.

Gone. _____

If I remember correctly, you didn't come to school the first week.

Where is this kid? I wondered.

When you finally arrived, I was pleasantly surprised. I learned about you quickly.

Your mom worked on a reservation, and it was quite a drive. She didn't love driving you to school in the morning, because she didn't leave for work that early.

Bus? No.

Walk? Most of the time.

Catch a ride? Nah.

You have so much potential. But you weren't about to hear that. Just like every other kid before you. Potential spilling out of their every pore.

Wasted.

Apathetic.

My first period class was enough to entice you for a while, but somewhere along the late fall...you showed up less and less.

If only they would let me pick you up. Why is that against the rules? You were willing, and I was able.

Uh...

teachers can't do that.

What if...

What if...

So, just like that, we let you fail. *You* let you fail. But you're 14.

WE let you fail.

So. Much. Potential.

H
is
for
Hopeful

I suspect you've known you were gay for a long time.

You stayed after one day to tell me. And you knew I already knew.

Your parents probably did too. But they wouldn't accept it. I hope that has changed.

I listened to you as you told me about your parents' beliefs, and how being gay was the ultimate sin. I wanted to hug you and tell you that it would all be okay.

For some it is. Okay.

They disown their families too, and find new ones to call their own.

For others, they end up on drugs, homeless, or selling themselves.

Or suicidal.

I cannot fathom, as a parent, thinking these things would be

better

than

a

gay

child.

I think you have found the right friends to be open with. They support you.

You are one of the countless reasons I try to maintain a

Safe classroom.

Hate is never welcome in my room.

You smiled when you left that day. I think I was the first adult you had come out to. And I loved you anyway.

I hope that mattered.

That tough girl exterior is a front.

We both know that.

I think I saw it break down when you sat in the back of my room and squinted because you didn't have glasses.

Pretty soon, you were hanging with the boys in my room. And talking.

Dad's been deported three times.

He's not coming back. Ever.

It's hard for you to even talk about him without crying. I can't even fathom how painful it was to have him ripped from your family.

Now it's just you, mom, and little brother. Crammed into a two bedroom apartment in a neighborhood that hears gun shots too often.

Your mom rented out one room to a couple. Common here, you tell me. So you sleep on a couch.

The brain in your head is your ticket out. You want to show your mom the world.

She deserves it, you tell me.

Somewhere into 9th grade you become interested in older boys, and I start to worry about you.

Riding in cars with boys.

Sex.

Drinking.

Smoking.

It's a path well-traveled in this town. Familiar. You'll wave to others you know here.

But what about your grades? Your ticket out of this town? Saving your mom?

You bounce from a fuck-them-attitude to a fuck-it-attitude every time we talk.

I tell myself it's the hormones, and being an angsty teenager. But angsty teens get pregnant.

And your ticket out ain't a baby, girl.

36

I

is

for

Intimidated

My first time as a student teacher was at a high school on the East side of the city I went to college in.

I was 22.

My cooperating teacher was a veteran, and had the utmost confidence in me...

Or she just wanted a break.

"It's better if you just start out by jumping right in."

We agreed on this.

I spent weeks pouring over lessons. I'd be teaching World Literature to Seniors. My classes were upwards of 40-45 kids.

There weren't enough seats. Or books.

The first day arrived and I was thrilled. I got out of bed, hadn't slept much, and was excited to get to school.

It hadn't *really* registered with me that I was a 22 year old, and my students were 18-19 years old.

All the preparing in the world hadn't prepped me for the attitudes I encountered the first day of school.

They were basically *my* age. They smelled blood, and went for the jugular.

"How old are you?" several of them asked.

Not only was there a severe bout of senioritis going around, but with a new teacher for 8 weeks, they thought they were on cruise control.

I quickly learned the way in which to pronounce my Hmong students' names. And that some of them were already married...to each other.

I learned that jumping into African literature sounded terribly boring and that bringing in all my trinkets, along with a plethora of food, from a recent trip to Africa changed their attitudes.

If I learned anything in those 8 weeks, it was that a little food goes a LONG way. Because it doesn't matter how old you may be, if you're offering treats...

They melt in your hand.

Title One schools are often gifted with free admission to events.

We saw basketball games, movies, museums, baseball games.

And, once, *Phantom of the Opera* on Broadway.

We boarded buses, and drove to Times Square.

I couldn't wait to see this epic show. On Broadway.

I had not been to a show with my students, and was pretty new to teaching in general, so I didn't prepare well.

These were the days before kids had cell phones in middle school, thankfully.

I didn't have much to worry about, right?

Wrong.

Hand-held Gameboys were shoved in to many pockets. And as soon as the house lights went down, the light glow of tiny screens came on.

I tried to keep the kids around me quiet, and the games from making noise, but it's not easy to scold kids in a dark theater.

Do you know how dark that play is?

I didn't either, until I turned around from my front-row balcony seat and saw nothing.

NOTHING.

Teachers from other schools a few rows over were appalled.

Ssh-ing could be heard constantly.

I was mortified, and thankful for the darkness.

At one point, a kiss.

And the cat-calling and whistles from my section could be heard over Times Square traffic, I was convinced!

At intermission, I was about to address my crew, when the theater manager approached me.

WHY DID I STAND UP?

"Excuse me, Miss? If you can't get these kids to quiet down, you'll all be asked to leave."

Other teachers, rows over, glaring as they watched this half-time show.

I have kids now, and they've thrown temper tantrums in public, and it doesn't even phase me. I don't think I will ever be as embarrassed as I was that day.

ROOKIE MOVE.

There was that time, when I first started teaching...

My first class.

I got married in October that year.

A rambunctious kid was annoyed with me one day.

"Yo, miss. Ain't you married?" he yelled.

Uh, yes.

"Then get up off *my* dick!"

Same kid. Different day.

Mom finally accepted the multiple invitations we had offered for her to come and sit with her son.

I hate to use the phrase, "Out of control," but his body would not sit in a desk all day. Instead he ran laps around my classroom in wild disregard for what others were doing.

A distraction, to put it nicely.

His mother showed up, in a tank top and painted-on-jeans. Slicked back ponytail with neck tattoos. Large name plate earrings in hoops. Nails, bright and long. She looked tough. Weathered by the neighborhood.

She appeared in my doorway and when I noticed, she made a "ssh" sign with her finger on her lips.

She wanted to watch him.

I complied. Who wouldn't?

Hell hath no fury like a pissed off Puerto Rican mother. She opened the door and the entire class froze.

SHE KNEW THEM ALL.

And down the line she went,

"Sit down! I'm calling ya motha. Pendejo!"

I asked if she wanted to come back every day.

J
is
for
Justified

I started buying groceries last year.
I didn't set out to do that, but when
I learned that a group of my boys
weren't really eating breakfast, or
anything much, I mentioned it to
my mom.

A few days later a huge box showed
up on my door step.

Granola bars, cereal, pretzels, fruit
snacks, juice boxes.

I cried when I opened the box. My
mom just gets it. I wish other
people did too.

Pretty soon I was feeding a group of
5-10 kids a day. They ate breakfast
or lunch in my room, and the rule
was that they had to work on
school work while they ate.

"You're crazy,"

I heard a few times.

But I heard "Thank you" even more.

Teachers are constantly subjected to visitors in their rooms.

I wonder, aside from doctors in residency, how often people are observed *doing* their jobs?

After I became a coach, I realized how valuable observations and visits can be. But I didn't forget how distracting it is to have adults with notebooks standing/sitting/kneeling in your classroom while you teach.

As I was a teacher with a nice-looking classroom, and I was compliant, and my class wasn't a shit-show most days, I was often asked if visitors could watch me.

I grew used to this.

Numb to it, actually.

I rarely received feedback, and never saw the people again, so what did I care?

If nothing, it kept me on my toes.

One particular visit involved a district superintendent, and other higher-ups, as well as teachers.

I prepared my students for the fact that we would have lots of people coming through.

Little did I know that it would be

All. At. Once.

13 adults.

13 extra bodies.

13 people with clipboards and notebooks and iPads.

13 extra distractions in a room full of kids who were already easily distracted.

I continued teaching. As you do.

At one point, however, as I walked around the classroom, I had to say,

Excuse me

To a woman who was standing in the middle of my room.

My Room.

My Kids.

I felt myself grow hot. Territorial.

Mama bear.

I shot my admin a look and they promptly knew it was time to move on.

I never saw them again.

No feedback.

Excuse me.

K
is
for
Kicked

My first time in the 18 story Department of Education building at 65 Court Street, in downtown Brooklyn, was for an interview.

The woman didn't believe I had worked with kids "from different cultures" before. She didn't even know where my state was on a map. She just knew it was a fly-over state. I literally had to prove I had taught brown kids! (She asked.) I showed her my shiny binder with pictures of Hmong, Somali, Native American students.

You're hired.

Come back for a job fair.

The job fair won't let me in, when I show up. Luckily the lady from HR is there, and escorts me in.

Go find a job!

I interview with a principal from West Harlem. Show up tomorrow morning for work.

The following morning, in a suit, I board a bus, train, and cab in a torrential downpour. It's hot. Because August in NYC is a sauna.

When I finally arrive, I wait. And wait.

No one comes.

Finally, excuse me. Were you here for the Language Arts position?

Yes, I say through dripping hair, and sweat.

I'm so sorry, but we just divided the courses up this morning in our meeting. We won't be needing you.

Fuck.

I call HR. They tell me to go to the holding room on 34th street.

The trains aren't running. Because, rain.

Manhattan and rain are a terrible combination if you need to get anywhere.

I pop out of the 4 train at 34th street and walk several blocks in the wrong direction. I haven't become accustomed to living as a gopher yet.

It's still raining. I'm sweating, crying, and my umbrella is broken.

I find the building. I find the room. It's littered with teachers. I learn quickly this is called, on the inside, the

Rubber room.

I sit. I am about to give up.

K?

Yes. That's me.

We don't have your paperwork. You'll have to go downtown to 65 Court Street.

But they sent me to you.

Well, I don't have papers for you. There's nothing I can do.

Back to the 4 train.

Brooklyn bound.

Again.

I show up in Brooklyn at 65 Court Street, again.

I must look awful. The rain, and sweat, and tears have ruined my makeup.

I don't even care anymore.

I sit on a chair, waiting for the HR person I originally was "hired" by to arrive.

She's at lunch.

Another woman walks by.

"Are you okay?" She looks horrified.

I quickly mutter my story.

The look on her face says it all.

Follow me, she says.

We walk into her office and I explain my journey. Literally *and* figuratively.

I just need this paper signed.

Unbelievable, she utters. Follow me, we're going upstairs.

That sounds important.

We go upstairs to a large office. The women in the office tell me to have a seat. They offer me stale animal crackers.

I realize I haven't eaten all day, and I look like a drowned rat.

Perhaps it was pity. Perhaps they were sick of stories like mine.

Were there others like me?

Why would anyone want to go through this to teach here? Aren't they begging for teachers in this place?

A woman signs my paper. She hands me a card. If you have problems, call me. Directly.

I leave, half wet. Half convinced I *can* live here.

But whole.

I still don't have a job. We don't have an apartment. I'm wet. But I arrive at our friend's apartment feeling like, maybe…just maybe things could work out.

It's a love-hate relationship, living here, our friend says.

Truer words have *never* been spoken.

In the morning, I get a call from Mr. Principal.

We spoke at the job fair. I can't hire you because my enrollment dropped. You should call Mr. Other Principal. He was the man sitting next to me at the fair. He has a position and wants to hear from you.

I call. We chat. He asks me to come to Brooklyn. Another trek.

But the sun is out and today is

new.

I learn about the school. It's

new.

Nothing

about it is new, save the name.

The guy is cool. He temporarily offers me a job on the steps of the elementary school we'll share a building with.

He's smoking a cigarette.

I don't know what a temporary offer means, but he says he'll know on the first day of school.

Just show up. I *should* know by noon that day.

I could have skipped home, but I still didn't have one.

First day of school.

I show up.

I meet no one.

Mr. Other Principal, who smells like a fresh cigarette and whiskey, walks me to my classroom. There are children in it.

There are no adults.

It literally looks like a zoo inside.

The kids are running in circles, jumping off desks.

This is 7th grade? I ask.

They *sort of* stop when we walk in.

Mr. Other Principal says, GOOD LUCK.

That's familiar.

Here we go.

L
is
for
Lonely

Your parents aren't together. And they had you at 15.

You spend a lot of time on your own, escaping the realities of living in a house with 10 too many people.

15 people lived there the last time I asked.

And teachers wonder why you don't get your homework done. Ha! Where the hell is that going to happen?

I've seen you at the soccer games. You want to play, but owe money from last season. I wish more than anything that I could pay it for you.

Uber has become your best friend.

You can get all over town and be everywhere and nowhere at the same time.

It must be lonely.

You laugh at everything. Your eyes always shining.

"I'm fiiiiine," you assure me.

But I wonder how?

Can I take you home, feed you, give you your own warm bed to sleep in?

I wonder if you'd even sleep in a house that was quiet at night, with a full belly.

Without worry.

I met you in 10th grade and we became connected quite quickly. You were a smart-ass jock.

You made me laugh, and refused to take me seriously.

A leg injury from basketball left you hanging in my room during lunch, and we shared plates of microwaved pizza rolls.

You'd written me a letter on your first day of class, as all my students do, and you…

Kept it.

When I told you I was moving back to NYC, you were mad. And when I jumped in the moving truck on a June morning, you'd driven to my house in the middle of the night and placed the note on my windshield.

MOVING.

We stayed in touch, and you've become one of my best friends.

We're oddly different, and yet can hang effortlessly.

You're challenging. Head strong. Stubborn as a damn mule. And really fucking brilliant. Beautiful in ways you don't even understand.

I want to pave the way for you. But you insist that I sound like a mom.

I *am* a mom.

You want to live your 20's the way you want. But you're sad.

And I was married in my 20's, you remind me.

How can I help?

Besides remind you,

And myself,

That you're in your 20's and it's hard sometimes.

Broken hearts hurt.

But like the wise elder, I know…

This too shall pass.

And I'll keep reminding you of our favorite line from The Kite Runner,

For you, a thousand times over.

You were in my first real class. I had no idea how to handle you. That sounds bad, but I just didn't.

So angry.

Crying.

Outbursts.

Refusals to do work.

I know so much more now, and for that I am so utterly sorry.

Textbooks don't teach teachers about girls like you.

We spent two years together. I moved with you to 8th grade, in part, because I was so connected to all of you.

Your world must have swirled around you then. You were always so frustrated. It was all

So confusing.

A force to be reckoned with, you were.

Strong.

I was scared one night when we played a basketball game that erupted in a fight. I shoved you all through a door and made you sit on the floor and breathe. The other side of the door being pounded on, and you all wanting out so you could kick some ass.

You were 13.

And you were ready to go.

I'd never seen anything like this before. It was

Terrifying.

Fighting with wild abandon. No cares about consequences, of any kind.

You became a young mother, to a beautiful little boy.

He looks like you, with huge, laughing eyes.

And then another one, but you lost him. I don't know why.

But your heart broke.

And mine broke for you.

If there was anger before, I can't imagine burying your newborn made that any better.

M
is
for
Miserable

In the fall of 2008 I went to work at a middle school in a nameless neighborhood in Brooklyn.

I didn't even know that neighborhood existed. Most don't.

When I get off the train, I have to stumble a few blocks *away* from the water.

Soon, I'm met by stacks upon stacks of projects. Public housing. It literally looks like Lego towers plopped down by a toddler.

I wonder why City planners thought this was such a good idea so long ago. Let's put *all* the poor people in the same, cramped, location.

Nothing good this way comes.

When I walked into the school, orientation day for the new teachers, there were 14 teachers sitting at desks.

14.

FOURTEEN!

The school had less than 300 students. That was over half the staff.

My gut told me to run, but I sat down instead.

I should have run.

K, you're wanted in the principal's office.

Words I've literally never heard.

This woman terrified me to my core. She was the starring act in all of my nightmares that year.

I should have run.

I walk in, timid.

I'm *not* a timid person.

She sat behind her fancy desk, with all of her matching pieces surrounding her.

You work in a shit neighborhood, and you're surrounded by shining cherry-wood adornments.

I sit, *after* I'm instructed to.

"Do you know why I've called you in here today?"

I swallow. Hard. Rack my brain.

"I do not."

The state test scores came in.

"They did?"

Now I have the feeling I'm going to pee my pants. This is all too formal. It MUST be bad.

Without a smile, she looks me dead in the face:

Your scores were the highest in the *entire* school.

Huh?

"Oh." I'm not sure if I should apologize.

"Aren't you happy?" she breaks into a smile.

"Yes," I manage a smile.

So I'm not in trouble? Can my body stop shaking, please?

"I doubted you. I really did. Your teaching methods are *different*."

Where I come from, *different* has two meanings. This didn't sound like a compliment, but hey, I'll take it.

Wait, did you just say you doubted me? I feel like this conversation is happening as an echo, or with a delay. I'm slow to process, but I think this is the part where (in my head) I walk out while saying, FUCK YOU.

I don't.

I say thank you, *indifferently,* like the goddamn professional that I am.

When I started my first job at a high school in my home state, I learned I was pregnant a few months before.

I was horribly sick all summer.

I tricked myself into thinking that New Teacher Orientation would be a good way to forget about the morning sickness.

It was going well all morning, until the bus ride.

We'll be taking you on a bus tour of the district the mayor informed us, after welcoming us to the district.

We bounced around on a yellow school bus from school to school. We didn't get out.

It was August.

It smelled like diesel.

I rode with my head between my legs for the majority of the trip.

When we returned to City Hall to close out the day with the mayor, I decided to sit in the bathroom.

I thought if I just sat on the toilet with my face pressed to the cold, tiled wall, I could overcome.

I did it! I felt better. Time to join the ranks.

I stood up, started to walk out of the stall, did an about-face, and hurled

ALL OVER the inside of the bathroom stall.

When I went to wipe it all up, the bathroom was stalked with those brown, cheap paper towels.

UN-absorbent.

I think I used every last one.

On a plus note, I felt better.

Welcome to year 3!

We had a lock down once.

It was real.

A copy-repair man had gotten past our security officer, who was not at the front desk. He unknowingly walked right in the front door and up the steps.

Poor guy.

My overhead loudspeaker didn't work, so I was a bit taken-aback when the dean burst through my door and yelled,

WE'RE ON A LOCKDOWN!

I was scared. We were sitting ducks. I had no idea.

We crowded into the corner of the room. Out of sight.

It got hot. Fast.

"Miss! I don't feel well."

SSHH. You'll be fine.

B A RRRRRRRRRRRRRRRR FFFFFF

SCREAMS.

Hushing.

D

R

I

P

It covered 80% of the kids hovered in the corner.

The smell hit instantly. Acrid.

Mixing with sweat.

I wanted to cry. Laugh. Run out the door.

After 15 minutes, the door opened. Didn't you hear? The lockdown was lifted.

Are you kidding me?

N

is

for

Nervous

Dear Ms. K,

Please report to my office on blah, blah, blah. We'd like to discuss the project your class is working on.

Sincerely,

Admin.

I can't imagine what this is about.

I sit down.

Am I being punked?

"Tell us about the project your students are working on. They really seem to like it!"

Wait- I'm *not* in trouble?

It's still unclear.

I explain. I give details; I talk too much when I'm nervous. I laugh a lot.

They look relieved.

But still question what I'm doing that the kids would *like* the class project so much.

How can we get other teachers to get their students *this* engaged?

Perhaps approaching this topic differently?

I don't say this. Because...I'm a goddamn professional.

A man started blogging about the school I worked at.

He wasn't a teacher, but a radio personality. His sources were to remain secret.

His blogs started gaining attention, shedding light on the hell that was.

The principal became upset. But what could she do? It wasn't slander. She had no proof of where the information was coming from.

Things became tenser at the school.

If that was even possible.

The union was involved with our issues.

We were really struggling to find support. And when we finally found a union representative who was trying to help us, he dropped dead of a heart attack.

Unfortunate. He was too young.

And once again we were left to our own devices.

And then, get this, the blogger was brutally murdered one night in his apartment!

Imagine the rumors that started to fly at school!

What was she capable of? We were terrified.

Turns out, it was a fluke thing, and he was involved in some online dating situation.

But for a hot second...

O
is
for
Optimistic

I have a business, you told me.

A business?

Most of the time, around here, that means you deal drugs.

But you, clearly, are not a dealer.

Your face radiates happiness, and you hang out with a different crowd than the stoners.

I learn quickly that you inspire others around you. You learned from a father who struggled, but overcame.

Do you know how lucky you are? To have a father? To have parents that push you?

Statistics aren't everything. Around here though, what you have is

Statistically rare.

An anomaly.

I worry you'll push yourself too hard. Or that the first time you fail, it'll break you.

But I can't worry about that.

Keep conquering the world, young one. You are a beautiful human with so much spirit, it comes out of every pore.

Remember where you came from; *who* you came from.

And know that others around you are looking up to you to be a mentor, a life vest, a lift.

Their stories are not the same as yours. _____

While teaching a Women in Literature course, I decided to teach about derogatory language.

I met with my principal to tell him what I would teach during my observed lesson.

Surprisingly, he didn't seem too shocked.

I like to push boundaries. He'd figured this out.

Our school was fairly conservative.

He challenged me on the "why" for what I wanted to teach.

WHY?

I was upset, and then challenged.

And I taught one of the better lessons I have ever taught.

Teaching kids about why they think name calling, often, refers to a form of female.

Bitch. Pussy. Wimp. Weak. Fairy. Pansie. Cunt.

The conversation was on point.
Kids were into it.

And angered.

And appalled.

And when I asked *them* the big why, they said,

"We can't change it if we're not aware."

Truth.

After the lesson, I anticipated my admin would be uncomfortable.

He wasn't.

I wasn't.

He had learned something too.

The discussion in class flowed smoothly. He noticed.

And it wasn't that my kids did great, and I felt proud. That was a given. It was more that I needed the challenge, and I rose to it.

I thought about scrapping the lesson. After all, did I want to say "pussy" in front of a 60+ year old man? My boss?

Not really.

But I did it. And I'm glad I push boundaries in my classroom.

That's often when the learning happens.

Madly in love with your high school girlfriend. I see you kissing in the halls. I see you sneaking to your car to smoke a cigarette. Or just to leave early.

You showed up in a credit-recovery class I was begged-in-to-teaching.

After school.

"This is a last chance for some of these kids."

I fumble through a credit-recovery-after-school-put-in-your-time program. There are teen moms; there are rednecks; there are bad attitudes.

But you. You're funny. And completely over high school. You've got the world by the balls, or so you think.

You beg me to do an independent study with you, because you're short credits. I beg the admin to let me. I don't know why, but it feels silly to not let you graduate over a few credits.

I give you a book to read. To finish. And to write a paper about.

You actually do it.

"I've never read a whole book, cover to cover."

You're 18 years old.

The picture we take at your graduation is one of my happiest moments. And yours.

Because you went on to become an addict. And a father with that high school girl.

And we've lost touch, somewhat.

I don't suspect you ever imagined that the credit recovery would be the easiest *recovery* you went through.

The summer after our rookie year, my co-teacher and I begged to move up with our class. They were going to be the first 8th grade class.

We were granted permission.

Besides,

NO ONE else wanted to teach them.

We spent the summer in our new classroom. 5th floor.

With cockroaches coming out to see what we were up to.

NEW YORK HUMIDITY.

We made a library, with check out cards, for our kids. We bought clipboards, and had tables, instead of desks. We wanted them to feel special.

We had a system.

Unconventional? At the time, yes.

Everyone who walked into our room thought we were nuts.

Were we nuts? For wanting to meet the kids we knew SO WELL where they were?

It wasn't an easy year. Clipboards broke. Tears were shed.

We tried to yell less, and hug more.

P
is
for
Pride

I will always remember the way you shook your hair. It was black silk. It lay perfectly straight, smooth, and shining in a bowl cut on your head. Your bright, brown eyes always looked delighted.

Like you'd just played a trick on someone.

Often, you had.

I lost touch with you, until your sister showed up in my son's daycare class.

In you strolled. A man.

You told me you were joining the military. I was happy for you, and your mom looked proud.

You were getting out of this neighborhood. Leaving so many classmates behind.

Dead, in jail, or in line for one of those.

Who knew we would end up living on the opposite coast at the same time.

You, a Marine.

Married. With a beautiful daughter.

Proud doesn't begin to describe how I feel.

You're the feel good story.

I think it was hard for you to manage high school.

Hockey made that easier. Built in friends, and expected socializing.

A cute, socializing girlfriend helped.

You're shy, though. It couldn't have been easy.

And when she broke your 17 year old heart, you were lost.

Because not only did you not have her, but socializing was awkward for a bit.

I worried about you a lot. You would reach out, and sound hopeless.

We talked.

You

Fell

Apart.

But high school ended, as it does. And hockey took you to different parts of the country, including my couch for a bit.

And when I retrieved you from your bus on Canal Street, a tall kid in Chinatown, I could see you were getting your sea legs. You stood with your shoulders back a bit more, and chest out.

You laughed. And smiled.

And you went off to college. Played more hockey.

Met a girl, and bought a house, and asked her to marry you, on a mountain.

I wished back then, when I talked to you through your tears, that I could have shown you who you would become.

A man of his own accord. No need for the built-in-hockey-social-status. Just you.

Confident. Smart. And killin' it.

Q
is
for
Quiet

How do I know so much about you, but you rarely speak?

The quiet boys usually have the most to say?

Your mom just got out of jail?

"For drugs."

"Ah, yes. Drugs." It's always drugs.

You and your little brother live with your former-gang-member-father in a small apartment.

And you don't eat, or talk much.

Addiction runs in the family, and video games consume your nights. You don't sleep much either.

It's no surprise when you tell me you contemplate suicide a lot. It usually coincides with the beatings your father doles out.

What can he possibly know about taking care of two teens? He lived in his car for years, while you two were in foster care. You resent him for this.

He has you now, though.

Mom stops over to spend time with you on the weekend, but usually arrives with a suitcase and drama in tow. Your father can't stand her, and that's the one thing you two agree on.

Your posture tells this story, and although you are lanky and tall, your body is trying to swallow itself.

You want to disappear from every room you're in.

My heart physically aches when I watch you. I want to hug you and tell you that it's going to be okay.

I do this when I can.

You seem to have given up on yourself and everyone else, and I can't fix that.

My wish for you is that you'll grow up and out. You'll leave this place that hurts you and find your tribe. You'll live up to your potential and use that hurt to propel you forward.

I didn't know you long. You came in
quietly and didn't make a sound.
Your dark features were so petite.

You looked like a lost little boy. I
know that's why I felt I needed to
help you.

Mom lives up north. And you're
down here with your brother.

"My brother has a lot of, uh,
problems."

I never figured out what that
actually meant. But you weren't
quick to say too much.

Soon you were missing school. For
a week once. I worried sick about
you.

Grandparents were in a fight. You
moved an hour south and were
commuting to school with your
grandfather. Every day.

I just keep wondering why your
mom isn't here. Why is your
brother with your grandma? Why
are you commuting an hour each
way every day?

You say you sleep in the car, but
you look tired always.

You say you do your homework on
your way home. But it's never
done.

There is more to this story. But I'm
gone now.

And I feel like I just left
you...blowing around in the wind.

R
is
for
Rage

Another email invite to discuss something with Admin. I'm new here, so I guess I should tread lightly.

I've been in contact with the school counselors about several of our students. Mostly mental health issues.

Two counselors for too many kids. In an area full of transient families, poverty, immigration.

Yeah, two seems like plenty.

I'm grilled about why students tell me things.

Yes, you read that correctly.

But why?

I'm so taken aback that my answer comes off as defensive.

Because I'm their English teacher. They do a lot of writing for me. This happens a lot in my classes. Always has.

I can't fathom why this is a bad thing.

I can't wrap my brain around ignoring glaringly obvious issues.

I can't understand how we can sit in staff meetings and talk about **reaching** our kids **with teaching** techniques when we are ignoring their basic needs!

It's not our problem?

IT'S

EVERY

ONE'S

PROBLEM.

IT'S

EVERY

ONE'S

PROBLEM.

IT'S

EVERY

ONE'S

PROBLEM.

IT'S

EVERY

ONE'S

PROBLEM.

IT'S

EVERY

ONE'S

PROBLEM.

IT'S

EVERY

ONE'S

PROBLEM.

You told me years ago that you were angry.

You were angry at your family. At teachers. Peers. School.

Every. One.

I couldn't blame you. It's hard to walk through this neighborhood without getting angry sometimes, and I don't even live here.

I ride a train of privilege home every day at 3. You ride that same train in the opposite direction.

Back to yelling.

Fighting.

Alcohol.

Drugs.

I ask you if you can start writing for me. But really it's for you. Keeping all that anger bottled up inside leads most boys straight to bad decisions.

Ultimately jail.

You start writing. Skipping classes and sitting in my room and writing pages upon pages. The hate and red comes pouring out onto the page.

I get in trouble.

He's supposed to be in class.

But you won't go to other classes. You wander the halls, hang in the bathroom, cause problems.

My solution is to have you sit in my room, where it is safe. Quiet.

Do you ever have a quiet place? I imagine you don't.

8th grade ends and you disappear.

You danced with the devil for a few years. Snipits on Facebook had me worried about you often.

We've recently reconnected.

I had no idea how much our time meant to you. I just thought you probably liked skipping classes.

"I need to see you one day. You're the best teacher I ever had and you're always on my mind. You taught me a lot."

I'm not sure how true that could be. But if there is one thing I've learned all these years, it's that kids are listening even when I think they aren't.

I hope you hear me when I tell you this:

You are so much more than what has happened to you.

"They always fight," you tell me. And you smile, but it hurts. I can see past the smile and into your dark eyes. You're hurting.

I ask you this.

You say you think about killing yourself all the time.

We hug.

You feel trapped at home because your dad drinks and your mom fights with him. You go for walks with your little brother so he doesn't have to hear them.

You've sought solace in falling for girls who *need* you. Sex won't fix this, I tell you.

One day you didn't come to school and I learned that you were in the hospital. I cried because I could not reach you and didn't know where you were.

I learn you took a bunch of pills, and now you're in some room with no sharp objects.

Rumors sweep the school, and I hear the majority of them. I do my best to dispel what I can.

But this is middle school and the town isn't that big. You get a label and weird looks when you get back to school.

I hug you again. Over and over, and tell you that I am so glad you are back.

We talk, but not enough.

You run to girls who comfort you, and demand too much from you because they're coming from similar houses. Dads are not around-drinks too much-doesn't show physical love. But you do, and they love that. And they love you. And you need that.

It's a cycle.

Please don't get them pregnant, I beg of you.

It won't fix anything.

It's a cycle.

It's a cycle.

Silent. I hardly knew you were in my class some days. You said...

Nothing.

Then, all of a sudden, there you were. Hanging around my desk. Not really saying much. A haircut, that I noticed, perhaps pulled you out from behind a literal, black and wavy curtain.

And each day you rushed to finish your work. But no. I stopped you.

"Go write the truest thing you can tell me," I said.

And a few moments later you'd written a whole page.

Suicidal. I suspected.

Call it gut. Call it a mother's instinct.

Something told me you had something to tell me.

We talked that day, or maybe the next. You cried. Hard.

I went to the counselor with you, and I cried. Which, I don't do at work.

This wasn't work. It was me, watching a younger version of myself. Alone, on a hard chair, in the counselor's office. Being looked at like a freak. Or with pity. Hard to tell in the moment.

I was so scared for you. They told me they were sending you to Children's.

I was scared for you. I knew what that felt like, in that moment.

I gave you my number, in secret. ~~Some lines *must* be crossed.~~ Because I needed you to know that I wanted you to be okay.

You texted me a bit later and asked me to come to the clinic. You were scared.

I came, immediately.

I talked with your doctor and therapist. I smiled at your grandmother and aunt. They couldn't figure out why I would show up.

You attended therapy once a week and we would talk about it after.

And now we talk almost daily. I can't imagine losing you to suicide.

But a family riddled with abuse, drugs, prostitution, lots of smaller siblings to raise. No bed to sleep in. I can't even imagine.

I want to help you so badly, mijo.

Still.

S
is
for
Surprise

"Heyyyy, Ms! Remember me?"

You walk into my classroom in a full U.S. Navy uniform. You've never looked so grown, and yet you're still an 8th grader in my eyes.

The curse of being a teacher is seeing kids as kids, even as adults.

You were new to our school; I think you showed up in 8th grade. And you dove right in.

God were you trying! Constantly talking, and goofing around when you were supposed to be working. But you were never mean-spirited.

And for that I couldn't fault you.

And for that I couldn't dislike you.

And for that I probably scolded you more than I should have, because you clearly craved attention you weren't getting from somewhere.

Now you're standing before me, a grown man, dressed in white. You have the hat on and everything. You walked through East Brooklyn in a sailor's uniform, with your chin in the air.

"I wanted to come and show you that I'm in the Navy. I know I was a crazy kid, but look at me now!"

We hug. I'm in tears.

"You've always been my favorite teacher."

And just like that I am humbled to the floor.

How? I wonder.

I guess that's the thing with teaching. Even the kids you think you aren't reaching...

Are listening.

And now you're gone, and I'm sitting in my chair with tears streaming down my face.

That's one of the feel-good stories. I wish there were more.

79

While teaching at a tiny school in Brooklyn, I had access to almost nothing. We didn't have paper for copies, there was no supply room, and the text books were ancient.

I doubt there were more depressing schools in that district.

I decided to read a book to my class that I had recently finished.

Chains. By Laurie Halse Anderson.

The story is realistic fiction, and takes place in lower Manhattan during the Revolutionary War.

After I read the book, aloud, to my class, I was somehow granted permission to take my students to Manhattan.

We visited Wall Street, where the main character had lived. We visited Trinity Church, where the main character, a slave, had attended church.

We walked to the Battery, where the character, acting as a spy, passed notes to soldiers.

They day was beautiful, and the students were in awe.

We took a picture with the statue of George Washington in front of Federal Hall, where he was sworn in as president.

On the subway back to Brooklyn, a mere 1-2 stops, a few of my students were talking to me, and told me something I hadn't considered.

I had taken for granted that we lived in New York City, and the proximity of where they lived compared to where we had visited.

I assumed they had been there before.

"I've never been to Manhattan, Miss. Thank you."

T
is
for
Terrified

My first day of school, you stumbled into my room at 2:15. You sat in a chair and talked non-stop for at least an hour. It was the first day of school. Where did you come from?

You had a lot of questions about New York. About gangs. About drugs. About what I knew about all that.

You never speak in class, but when you're with me, you never stop.

I learn a lot. I learn about the divorce, and the dad who works a lot, trying to raise the four of you on his own.

I also learn about your drug habit, and the deals you're making on campus.

You've got this shit on lock. You won't get caught.

Your grades are going up and up. You walk with more confidence. You present a project to the class, and although you're playing it cool, I can tell how proud you are of yourself.

Because we worked on it for hours after school when no one could see you caring. Ssh.

I take you on a college visit one weekend. We walk around UC for 4 hours.

In awe. We both are. You with it. Me with you, and the naïve little boy you are.

And then the inevitable happens.

You get caught.

Admin doesn't want to tell me. They know it's going to break me. And it does.

POOF. Gone. You were just

GONE.

But we've connected in person a few times. You remember every little thing I have ever said to you.

When I visited last, you showed up at a park- in a truck, without a driver's license. In your colors.

So you could give me a hug and a piece of cheesecake from your recent birthday party.

A little boy in gangster's clothes. I can't help but cry over the juxtaposition.

And I do cry. In my car. All the way to my hotel. Because when I leave, I feel like next time you'll be behind glass or in a coffin. And I really just can't.

u
is
for
unsafe

The first year at my first school offered some opportunity.

The girls wanted a basketball team.

I could do that. My co-teacher agreed.

We could do that.

When we felt helpless, we could *at least* do that.

We practiced, a lot. It was the funniest thing we had ever experienced. The girls, products of a system that doesn't encourage female athletes, had never touched a basketball.

Eventually, they wanted a game.

My co-teacher talked with a classmate of hers who was doing the same thing we were.

What a great opportunity.

We thought.

They came to our gym. We were pretty unconventional. No security stayed. We were the only adults in the building.

About half way, or a bit more, through the game, with neighborhood fans cheering, one of our girls decided the jump ball was *hers*.

She wasn't giving in.

Nails came out.

S L A P P I N G.

And then, benches cleared. The fans joined in.

The three of us twenty-somethings-coaches were at a loss.

This was *not* going to end well.

S C R A T C H I N G.

P U N C H I N G.

S C R E A M I N G.

It felt like an eternity before I got our girls up the steps and into the cafeteria, behind a solid door.

The other coach got her players to the train, but were followed by our "fans"- hot pursuit.

I was appalled.

In all my years of playing basketball, nothing like this had ever happened.

Parents and cousins and siblings were banging on the door behind me. I was pushing it shut, thankful for my 6 feet.

"Back the fuck up!" I screamed.

Welcome to New York.

As most secondary teachers know, our duties are not only to teach upwards of 150-200 kids a day, grade all of those papers, and collect data from weekly assessments...we have "other duties" too.

These duties may include, but are not limited to: lunch duty.

Or as I like to call it: doody duty.

This is a part of the day that no teacher looks forward to.

After kids leave your classroom the last thing you feel like doing is heading to a contained area to listen to them scream.

Worse yet, is the outside duty.

In a contained yard. In a city.

Balls fly over fences, arguments break out over the use of the handball court, and small-menacing groups form (usually to protect the two kids making out in the middle).

Once, when I was not-that-visibly-pregnant, I was standing outside, trying not to puke (a new hobby). A large male, formerly incarcerated, man-child approached a boy standing near me. He started running his mouth.

The boy near me didn't stand a chance. And knew that, so he didn't say anything.

Instinctively, I stepped between them.

Pregnant.

The man-child swung

around me.

He connected with the kid I was shielding. The sound muffled, because on the way around my head, he hit my ear in the process.

It stung.

Not as much as the crack I heard when his fist connected with the boy's nose.

85

I was sitting with a teacher that I was coaching once.

Over the loud speaker we hear:

Attention staff and students. This is a *soft* lockdown. I repeat, this is a *soft* lockdown. Please lock your doors.

Does that mean we keep doing what we're doing? What's going on?

I didn't have time for a lockdown. I had another school to get to.

I went to the security desk to ask if I could go, or if they'd tell me what was going on.

Someone was just stabbed. Right out the front door.

OH.

I was able to leave a few minutes later. I guess they had removed the body. A kid. 17-ish?

Oh no. Did I know him? After all, this was the neighborhood I had taught in for years.

The crime tape was everywhere when I walked out the front door. Detectives.

They looked like they were filming another episode of True Bloods.

But there were no film permits hanging up.

V

is

for

violated

I feel like I failed you. The system most definitely failed you. Your family failed you. The school failed you. Will people fail you your whole life?

The black hair you wear around you like a veil was telling when you walked into my room. The lights seemed harsh to you, and you were almost-mute. Dying to disappear. I get it now.

That's why I was surprised when from out-of-nowhere, behind me, you're standing.

Something is wrong. "What's up?"

Crying. Snot pouring out of your nose. Down your chin. Tears in your hair, sticking to your face.

I didn't expect this. I don't know what to do or say. We've hardly talked much, and I don't understand what this is about. But you're here, in front of me and the entire class.

We have a muffled conversation, and I know what you're going to tell me before you say it.

Don't say it. Please don't be *that*.

The class leaves when the bell rings, and we sit there.

"He made me put it in my mouth."

No.

I've never felt so sick. I try to remain calm, for your sake and mine.

But all I want to do is throw up. And punch something. And scream.

"And my sister too."

No.

No.

And CPS does nothing because it isn't happening anymore. It was in the past.

"There was more than one," you say. "They knew my dad."

MANDATED REPORTER.

I do what I have to do. What I am *obligated* to do.

But nothing I do will ever take the dick out of an eleven year old's mouth.

T

This is another one of *those* stories

The one you hope isn't true.

A family friend.

He forced.

You complied, because, well, you were in 7th grade.

It just about destroyed your family. Your father lost his job because that "friend" was his boss.

A slut. Your brother calls you that when he's mad. You know it's not true, but...

When you hear something often enough, it drips like honey into your brain. Starts to coat your thoughts. You try to shake it away, but it sticks to other thoughts.

They know it's not my fault, but it feels like they are blaming me.

Parents fighting.

Brother fighting. Smoking.

So your dad leaves, and you go with him. Head east. To find work.

I'm not sure why.

Eventually you come back. Find a boy.

Start to lie. Spend nights with him.

I've never comprehended why girls who get raped find solace in other men. Not all do, but you are.

It worries me. Sex is not sacred anymore?

I mean, I guess. Why would it be?

Quit the smoking, pick up the guitar, girl. Your fingers will hurt, but your heart won't break again.

W
is
for
Wise

I don't think life was easy for you in middle school.

Although you are Puerto Rican, you didn't have the *right* look for many of your classmates. That pale skin and those freckles were not easy to contend with.

Being a bookworm was your safe haven, but again, didn't do you any favors in middle school. It simply made you a nerd.

There are scars on your arm where you once etched your pain.

I won't forget that twinkle in your eye, or your sharp-tongued comments when other kids were goofing around in class.

At home, a single mom. A brother who required a lot of attention.

Wise beyond your years.

You're a proud feminist-lesbian now. I suppose you always were, but I'm glad you're out. You seem so happy, and that twinkle is still there.

I'm beyond proud of you for getting through that period in your life, in a neighborhood that doesn't appreciate a good education, book nerds, or white girls who "aren't".

I taught a College Prep class once, to high schoolers.

I hadn't taught such a class before, and was really trying to give it my all.

After the students had finished their first drafts of papers, I decided that I should give them feedback.

The papers were long.

I started on Friday afternoon and finished Sunday night.

My hand hurt, my eyes were crossed, and my red pen was out of ink.

I had given feedback on every page of every paper. I corrected periods and commas. Every. Damn. Error.

The following Monday, I handed papers back, asked kids to make the edits, and turn in Final Drafts to me on Wednesday.

Please attach the rough draft.

When I received the papers back, I started reading through the pile. I assumed it wouldn't take long because all they had to do was edit what I told them to edit.

The first paper I read looked **exactly** like the draft. I was mad.

The second paper looked **exactly** like the draft. I was more mad.

The third paper. The fourth paper.

ALL THE FUCKING PAPERS!

Not one kid had changed one error.

The wrath of a deity I don't even believe in, could not compare to how angry I was. I felt duped.

That said, they weren't getting the last laugh. NO SIR.

I walked in the next morning and didn't say a word. Instead, I passed out tissues.

One girl asked, "Is this because we are going to cry when we get our papers back?"

DING DING DING!

I kept my face pleasant while handing out all the big red F's on the papers.

Is it cold in here, or is it just me?

Interestingly enough, not one kid dared to contest their grade.

They knew.

---

x
is
for
x'd out

I sat in a staff meeting on the last day of school. I'd taught there for several years. I'd weathered every storm we'd had, from the beginning.

Assignments for the upcoming year were being handed out.

I got the paper last. I could feel people looking at me. My face grew hot.

My name was not listed under "English Language Arts"

It was listed as the SAVE ROOM teacher. The SAVE ROOM is for the kids who want to be assholes. They can't be suspended, so they get stuck in a room for the day. It's like a daycare center, but kids do not want to be there.

NO ONE had prepared me for this.

NO ONE said, Hey, you'd be good at this.

NO ONE informed me they were going to fuck me over. In front of every one of my colleagues, no less.

They awaited a reaction, but I *knew* that's exactly what they wanted. I wouldn't give it to them.

I WILL NOT CRY IN SCHOOL.

I managed to get to my neighbor's room before I burst into tears.

NO ONE could understand what was happening.

I'd learn later what really happened. That didn't save me any face though.

I was begged to take on the role- the role they knew I didn't want.

I have a Master's degree. I'm not a fucking babysitter, I told them.

They knew.

Want to teach Science?

Yes. Yes I do.

Y

is

for

Youthful

A school I was coaching at a few years ago had three floors. The teacher I worked with there was on the third floor.

I walked in and up the stairs, like usual. I took one step into the hall and almost fell.

SLICK. SHINING.

What happened to the floors? I asked, while sliding my way to her door.

The 8th graders played their "senior" prank.

Baby oil.

O N

      E V E R Y

         F L O O R.

Slick is right.

Earlier that year the floors were shining for a different reason. They had been washed really well.

"Good thing you weren't here yesterday."

A kid punched the wall. He was mad.

The bone in his arm decided to pop through his skin, you know, for *full effect.*

The blood sprayed everywhere. He freaked out and ran up and down the halls.

BLOOD EVERYWHERE.

My co-teacher and I decided to teach a unit on explanatory writing. We wanted our students to understand how to give directions, thoroughly, in their writing.

Instead of writing boring papers on how to make a peanut butter sandwich, we told them we were having a tv show where they would have to demonstrate the directions they wrote.

We were very excited for this day, as our students had been writing drafts and final papers for a week. We hung a huge sheet of butcher paper from the ceiling and set the chairs up a like a studio audience in front of a green screen.

They were ecstatic.

The kids brought in peanut butter and celery to make ants on a log. They demonstrated pitching a baseball, shooting a jump shot, and braiding hair.

The final student, a hyper-active, incredibly charismatic, fast talking Dominican boy demonstrated bachata dancing.

My kids were either Dominican or Puerto Rican. The few that were not, knew these dances anyway because they lived in this neighborhood.

The demonstration morphed into an all-out dance off in the middle of the room.

They danced the salsa.

They danced the bachata.

They danced the merengue.

I was impressed.

And then they asked me to dance.

This boy, demonstrating for me, grabbed my hips and said, "Like this."

Apparently, it wasn't working.

"Miss, you move your hips like a *white* girl!"

Many districts have gotten away from celebrations of any type of holiday.

It's just easier.

In one of my schools, this wasn't the case. And I loved it.

One year I decided that the entire school should have the opportunity to see Manhattan in December.

If you haven't. Go.

It doesn't matter if you subscribe to a particular religion, or not. Manhattan in December is magical.

A lot of our students had never seen it.

I created a scavenger hunt to find all things-holiday from 59th street to 34th street.

Groups were assigned. All staff participated. We had groups of about 10-15 kids and we took to the streets. Some started at 34th street first. Some at 59th.

If you don't know, 34th street is where the OG of Macy's stores is.

THE Macy's. With its wooden escalators, in house candy and coffee shops, and most importantly,

SANTA.

The group I led was a group of my 8th graders. We started by counting the Christmas trees outside of the Plaza hotel. We took pictures. We saw the Unicef Star hanging over 5th Ave.

We went into Trump Tower and saw the indoor Italian marble waterfall. The kids took pictures with the doormen.

We looked at all the windows along 5th Ave.

We arrived at Rockefeller, freezing, and excited. We took a group picture in front of the tree.

I was nervous about bringing them to Santaland. 8th graders? Santa?

We walked, and walked, and walked. They were cold.

When we arrived at Macy's, we took the wooden escalators up to the 8th floor. I explained that these were some of the first stairs like this in the country. They were original.

We walked into Santaland and wove through the trainsets, and dancing dolls. We saw sparkles, and lights, and smelled cinnamon.

And when it was our turn to see Santa…

I witnessed kids in sagged jeans, hoodies, large headphones, iPhones; too cool…turn to children. Forget the city, THIS was magical.

I'll never forget the day our kids were all working. It was like a movie.

I had a small group.

My co-teacher had another.

Some

     kids

          were

               scattered

     reading

All over the room.

And then a scream!

"They're FUCKING!" a boy yelled, who was reading by the window.

The window that overlooked the entire New York skyline.

We had the best view.

So did he-

Of the high schoolers who snuck up to the roof of the projects in the middle of the school day.

An administrator ran to my room to find out what the commotion was about.

I told her what was going on.

She shrugged.

Not much you can do about that, huh?

She smirked, and walked away.

I'd never seen her smile before.

z
is
for
zany

Another kid who didn't really speak in class.

You seemed a bit out of place at the time, but not.

Nothing about you stood out, but your silence.

I had no idea. None.

We weren't close, really. But you intrigued me.

After high school you moved west. You found your niche.

Bisexual. Raving. Leather and bondage, maybe? Hmm...that seemed out of place.

But that's it. You conformed just enough to fit in to your little town, where none of that would have been accepted.

But you left. And you found yourself.

And I couldn't be more proud of the woman you've become.

Your talents are too big for where you came from. You were smart enough to know that and leave.

How many kids don't? _____

Reckless. Unafraid. Bold.
Unapologetic. Gorgeous.

Reckless.

And so fucking smart.

But college didn't set you on a path
for success.

Parents divorcing. No co-signers for
a loan. You were out on your own
in a world you weren't prepared
for.

I attempted to scoop you up and
save you. I didn't do my best; I
know this.

You took to the city and I thought it
would be the best place for you.

Fresh. New start.

No more drugs.

Get a job, put one foot in front of
the other. School can wait.

But you flew the coop. Back to the
shit storm you left.

Soon a call I was hoping I wouldn't
get. Pregnant.

No.

But a miscarriage.

Then, silence. I didn't hear from
you for a long while.

I wish you could see what I'm
looking at when I look at you.

I've avoided seeing you recently,
because I'm scared.

I don't want to be another adult
giving you the get-your-shit-
together rhetoric, but inevitably,
that's what I want to say.

Women like you are special. You
could have the world by the balls.

Bartending and partying and drugs
aren't going to get you to where
you are capable of going.

30 comes fast. As fast as 25 did.
And then it's not a party anymore.

It's not fair, losing your father to a
liver that hardened under the stress
of life.

There are other options, you know.
I know you know.

Do you know?

People get confused when I call them "my" kids, because I do have my own birthed-children. But when you spend the amount of time with kids like I have, then pronouns change.

I've shared in their happiness, fears, sadness, frustrations.

Some people ask me why I do this job.

Shit, some days I ask myself the same question.

But all I have to do is think of the A-Z kids.

My kids.

The stories I have.

I can smile or cry thinking of kids I still know and talk to. Who have allowed me to be part of their lives...still.

And no. I won't save them.

But I won't give up on them either.

A call to action:

Perhaps these stories have left you with several of your own emotions to grapple with. It is my hope that this is true. If you feel like those emotions compel you to do something, rest assured, there is plenty to be done.

Talk to the kid that doesn't get invited over. See if he's hungry. See why he's hungry.

Ask the teacher you know, because we all know a few, if they need anything for their classrooms. In December. And again in the Spring.

Save your Box Tops and bring them to a school, if you don't know a kid to give them to.

Volunteer to tutor, read, play games, coach- at a school, library, youth center.

Start a garden at the school in your neighborhood.

Write to your local politicians and ask them to fund and fight for public education.

Donate to shelters in your area. There are lots of kids who go to shelters each night.

Offer to come to the school on Career Day and talk about what you do.

If you own a business, donate to the schools.

If you own, or work in, a place that could offer field trips...do that. Offer them.

Don't throw out your crayons, glue, markers, paper, toilet paper tubes, 3 ring binders, pens...someone needs them. They are better in a kid's hand, than in a landfill.

Ask a local sports club if there are kids that need scholarships. Or shoes. Or gear.

There is a lot to be done.

I hope you feel inspired to go and make the world a better place.

Gratitude—

First, thank you to the hundreds of students who have shared their lives with me. For trusting me. For letting me in. You are the reason I continue to teach, and for why I get excited on my way to school each day.

Thank you to my parents, for believing in me. For listening to my stories. For reminding me why I do this job on the days it feels like I can't anymore. For believing in me, always.

Thank you to the friends who have read the drafts of this book and have encouraged me to keep writing.

Thank you to the countless teachers I've worked with who have helped me get through the best days and the worst days. This career is no joke.

And finally, to the loves of my life. Thank you Munchie and Squish for being the most amazing kids. My love for you is infinite. Thank you for sharing me with all of my kids, the others, whom you've come to know. And to my one true love, I'd have given up a hundred times by now if it weren't for your support. Thank you for listening, believing in me, and being my rock. You truly are the best friend I'll ever have.

The End.

k.a. campion can
be found on
Instagram am
@hisforhumanby
k.a.campion

Thank you for
following!

Made in the USA
Lexington, KY
20 September 2017